The Story of *Craft* Beer

Pete Brown

Contents

My Story
James Brown, Founder of Beer52

My adventure in craft beer began on a road trip on the back of my Dad's Harley-Davidson motorbike. We travelled around Europe together, discovering great small breweries along the way. Stopping for beers throughout Belgium, we realised that we were drinking beers that we wouldn't be able to find again when we went back home.

The idea for Beer52 was born – I would start a craft beer club, exploring the beers of a new country each month. After getting my friend Fraser on board for the ride, we set out to create our first selection of beer. Having enjoyed

a few nights of tasting great beers together, we settled on a group of our favourite local breweries to bestow our inaugural case with their beers.

From these humble beginnings, it's been a journey that has taken us throughout Europe and as far away from home as the west coast of the USA, in search of awesome beers for our members. Our team has grown to more than a dozen awesome craft beer enthusiasts, who help to make our community of tens of thousands of drinkers tick.

Remarkably for such a young company, we were named the "UK's Best Independent Craft Beer Retailer" by SIBA, an award that we put down to the simple fact that we only sell beers that we like to drink ourselves.

We've brought beers to the UK that have never before been on sale in the UK and even collaborated with some of our brewing heroes to create exclusive beers for the club. Some of the highlights have included spending time with the likes of Stone in California and Mikkeller in Denmark, finding ourselves at the very heart of the worldwide craft beer movement.

We've worked with everyone from 'punks' (Brewdog) to monks (Westmalle) and everyone in between. The one-

man-band brewers operating out of an industrial unit in Manchester to the grandfathers of the IPA on the American west coast. The experimental Danish 'beer architects' at To Øl to the winemakers-turned-brewers at Firestone Walker.

Some people ask us, 'Surely it gets boring visiting hundreds of breweries – aren't they all the same?'. Well, sure the tanks aren't all that different from place to place, but the people and their beers sure as hell are unique at each place we go. The opportunities to experiment with recipes and ingredients are limitless with beer – not to mention the plethora of different hop varieties and yeast strains that offer the brewer a vast palette of flavour profiles to explore.

For us, craft beer offers a whole world of styles, tastes and histories to discover and, having tasted several thousand different beers at this point, we feel like we're still only just getting started. When this all began for us four years ago, we found all of this variety pretty overwhelming. So, now, we figured it would be a great idea to put some of what we've learned into a handy little book for you.

It's a book that we wanted to be fun and easy to read – so who better to write it for us than our very own *Ferment* contributor, Pete Brown?

James Brown
Founder, Beer52

Introduction

Bob Monkhouse had a brilliant one-liner that went: "When I told people I wanted to be a comedian, they just laughed at me. Well, they're not laughing now."

Being a beer writer is nothing like being a comedian. Not intentionally, anyway. But even though the logic of the gag doesn't translate, when I think back to the dark days when I first started writing about beer, I can't help but emulate Monkhouse's fake-smug impression when he says, "They're not laughing now."

About five minutes ago, beer used to be a bit of a joke. It was boring and bland, and it was dull and farty, and was only drunk by old men with beards (ale) and football hooligans (lager). That last sentence is completely untrue. But that's how beer was portrayed, and how most people were happy to see it. Saying you wrote about beer usually prompted spluttering laughter from people choking on their chardonnay.

Over the last twenty years, we Brits got increasingly interested in flavour, ingredients and provenance in our food and drink. And eventually, it became bizarre that beer was the only product that seemed to be an exception to this. When the change came, it was all the more dramatic for having been bottled up for so long. The rise of social media, the search for something different and interesting, the realignment of priorities caused by the global financial crash of 2008, and the coming of age of a new generation who looked at the increasingly dishonest promises of a corporate career ladder and thought "Fuck that, I'm doing something for myself, something I care about," were just some of the factors that came together to create the current British beer boom.

Whether you call it 'craft' or not, and what you mean by that particular c-word, it doesn't really matter. The revival of old traditions, the liberation of viewing those traditions and recipes as inspiration for creativity rather than religious texts and the shrinking, increasingly inter-connected world that has brought everyone else's traditions and innovations to our doorstep, mean we now have more brewers in Britain than in the 1930s, and more different beer styles and flavours than we've ever had.

There's never been a better time to be a beer drinker in Britain, but all this choice, all these styles, can often seem a little bewildering. How much do you really need to know about hops? What if you get bored of them? What other beers are there if you didn't like them in the first place? And, come to think of it, what exactly are hops and what do they do in beer? How can you have a black IPA when IPA stands for 'India Pale Ale'? And if it's called India Pale Ale, why is it made in America?

We're guessing you don't want to spend too much time pondering these questions, but that you're idly curious about at least some of them. That's why we've given you this small book. It's a short read. If you do, you'll learn a lot about beer. And if it leaves you with more questions than when you started, consider this the start of a journey of discovery that will always be more fun with a glass in hand.

Cheers,
Pete Brown

The Story of *Craft* Beer

How the world's favourite beverage evolved from porridge to barrel-aged citra-hopped hibiscus saison.

No one really knows when beer was first brewed. As the technology aiding archaeology develops, the likely first evidence of brewing pushes further and further back in time. The current best estimate is that mankind enjoyed its first beer around 7,000BC. That could go even earlier, but the cut-off limit is likely to be around 10,000BC.

We've always enjoyed a drink. Alcohol occurs naturally and we're not the only animals who like it. The 'Drunken Monkey' theory of evolution even suggests that our taste for booze helped us evolve and survive, because primates who are attracted to the smell of fermenting fruit get to the juicy goodness first.

But while we may have been drinking the forerunners of wine and mead for tens of thousands of years, beer is made from grain, and that grain needs to be modified before it can be brewed into beer, and that modification requires specialised equipment and buildings. Beer is likely as old as the first permanent settlements, and brewing may be the reason we first decided to build those settlements.

At a time when most people would have lost their teeth by adulthood, beer was an easy way to ingest calories and vitamins, and has long been a source of food as well as drink. And here's a secret: beer also makes you feel pleasantly intoxicated. This sensation made our ancestors feel closer to their gods, so beer had a big ceremonial as well as dietary role.

By the time of the earliest recorded writings, beer was fundamentally important to society. One of the earliest ever examples of writing is the 'Hymn to Ninkasi', a paean to the goddess of beer that also serves as the oldest surviving beer recipe, written down in ancient Sumeria in around 1800BC, but no doubt much older in the oral storytelling tradition. Since then, beer has been indispensible to any society around the world that has grain growing nearby.

The Egyptians also had a beer goddess, placed beer in the tombs of dead kings to sustain them in the afterlife, and even used beer as currency to pay people.

Beer at this time was a porridge-like substance with the grains still in the mix, and was drunk through long straws. The longer the straw, the more people could fit around the pot. Drinking beer has always been a communal, shared experience.

For most of history, beer also meant home brew; brewing was a domestic activity, like baking, until just a few centuries ago. In the UK, brewing gradually moved to alehouses, and some of these began to supply their neighbours, giving rise to the 'common brewer'.

But it wasn't until the Industrial Revolution that big brewers emerged. Those who took early advantage of new technologies such as steam power and innovations such as the microspore and hydrometer grew rapidly from the eighteenth century onwards, benefiting from economies of scale and reducing prices, until most pubs realised they could buy beer more cheaply than they could brew their own.

Large-scale brewing also gave us the first modern beer styles. Porter became the drink of eighteenth century Britain, and later gave birth to stout. The thirst for good beer in the British colonies saw stock ales, designed to keep well, evolve into India Pale Ale (IPA), which in turn evolved into lighter pale ales for the domestic market. IPA ruled the world until Czech and then German brewers took pale ale's malts and combined them with German lager yeast and Czech and German hops to create pilsner lager. Pilsner appeared just before refrigeration and rail transport, and took advantage of both of these to sweep the planet.

Pilsner prompted the second wave of consolidation among brewers. Again, those who invested first in big conditioning tanks and the new yeast cultivation technologies of the 1880s grew bigger than ever, and the rest got left behind. Here and there, in Belgian monasteries and British towns, some resisted lager's dominance, but by the mid-20th century, imitation pilsner lager was the world's favourite beer, and has remained so ever since.

When brewers floated on stock markets to fund yet bigger expansion, their focus inevitably shifted from brewing great beer to ensuring returns to shareholders. After two hundred years of technology being applied to improve beer quality, from the mid-twentieth century most new advances were about cutting corners, cutting costs, cutting lagering time and cutting ingredients.

The death of good beer played out slightly differently on either side of the Atlantic. In Europe, old brewing traditions clung on as niche interests, with Belgian abbey, Trappist and saison ales and British real ale becoming increasingly archaic, associated with older generations.

But in the United States, the prohibition of the 1920s wiped out old brewing traditions altogether. When beer flowed again in the 1930s, it became increasingly bland, increasingly interchangeable. The 'beer wars' of the 1970s, fought with huge TV ad campaigns, saw a rapid consolidation of the market until three brands – Budweiser, Miller and Coors – controlled around 80 per cent of the beer market, all selling faux-pilsner lagers.

But it was from this dire situation that the fight-back started. When prohibition was repealed in 1933, a simple administrative oversight meant that home brewing remained illegal. Correcting the mistake remained a low priority for successive administrations, and it wasn't until 1979 that President Jimmy Carter finally legalised homebrew again.

Free to brew their own beer at last, the last thing Americans wanted to create was lager like the Big Three made. They were crying out for flavour, and they looked across the Atlantic to find it.

The problem with brewing good lager is that it needs to be stored cold for several weeks while it matures, and this was beyond the resources of most home brewers. So instead they turned to ale, particularly the classic and almost forgotten old English beer styles like porter and IPA.

With no tradition of their own to uphold, the Americans were free to combine tradition with experimentation. The beers they made were flavourful and robust, and it wasn't long before some of them were moving from their garages and basements to open small-scale commercial breweries.

When Ken Grossman and Paul Camusi pulled together a bunch of discarded dairy equipment and scrapyard metal to create the Sierra Nevada brewery in 1979, they first attempted to brew classic British styles. But stuck in California, they couldn't get access to the precious Fuggles and Goldings Kentish hops that characterised English real ales. Instead, they had to make do with Cascade hops, grown in the American Pacific North West. As a result, they utterly failed to create a beer that tasted like their beloved English ales. But the beer they'd ended up with instead became Sierra Nevada Pale Ale.

This was the beer that became the lodestone for American craft brewers. No one had tasted a beer with such a distinct aromatic hop character before, and other brewers rushed to copy it, for the first time really exploring the aromatic properties of hops rather than simply using them for bitterness. The realms of hoppiness were pushed so far, so quickly, that Sierra Nevada Pale Ale is now classed as an 'English-style pale ale' by the American beer judging fraternity, even though its hop character is far bigger than anything available in Britain until much more recently. American-style IPA combined recipes written for the East India Company with American aroma hops and modern brewing technology to create a new style of beer that won new fans. People who thought they didn't like beer were won over by its aromatic pungency and bitter buzz.

IPA became the shop window of the new American craft beer movement; hardly any of America's 5,000 breweries don't brew at least one. The style developed, with stronger double IPAs then eventually leading to experimental black IPAs and hybrids with other styles.

Spurred by this success, American craft brewers raided the bank of half-forgotten European beer styles, recreating and reimagining porters, stouts, barley wines, Belgian abbey and saison beers, wheat beers, German Kölsch-style beers, bocks, pilsners and amber lagers.

Back in Britain, real ale remained an ageing niche, as drinkers increasingly turned to big global lager brands, eventually growing bored of beer altogether, abandoning pub culture for home entertainment, drinking less, and turning to wine and cocktails when they still did.

What seemed increasingly odd as Britain began to embrace a much more foodie culture – seeking out quality and variety in bread, cheese, meat and vegetables, elevating chefs to superstar status and filling shelves with cookery books – was how boring old beer seemed increasingly to be the only food and drink that wasn't part of this revolution. When the change finally came, it was all the more dramatic for having been bottled up so long.

Like any revolution, craft beer happened in Britain thanks to several different things all coming together at once.

First, on the industry side, the introduction of Progressive Beer Duty in 2002 made it much easier to open and run a small-scale brewery. The number of brewers in Britain began to increase, even though for a time, most were brewing interchangeable best bitters and golden ales.

Second, in terms of demographics, a new generation reached drinking age. For so-called millennials, the lagers their parents drank were dull and boring, and real ale re-emerged as a novelty, freed from the previous generation's negative views.

And then, social media arrived. Denied any coverage in mainstream media, beer bloggers made the internet their own. A lively community of writers, brewers and retailers set up an intimate environment where ideas were discussed and events planned. People began to learn about American craft beer and the hops that were driving it. Slowly, American craft beers became more available in the UK. And British brewers such as Thornbridge and Dark Star began to get their hands on American hops and make British beers with them, sometimes in collaboration with the US brewers who pioneered then.

Facebook and Twitter went mainstream just around
the time smartphones made the whole medium mobile.
This was perfect for beer: the permanently ongoing
conversation, sometimes local, often global, could now
take place in real time in the pub or bar, with brewers
writers and drinkers meeting up simultaneously on- and
off-line. When BrewDog launched in 2007, it built its
entire notorious brand via social media, creating a new
and very successful business model that inspired countless
others to follow its lead, bringing the language, imagery,
attitude and flavours of American craft beer to the UK.

While this was happening, the world was reeling from the
global financial crash, and this provided the final spark for
the craft beer boom in several important ways.

First, commercial property in cities, especially in London,
became much cheaper. In 2006 it simply didn't make
commercial sense to think about opening a small brewery
in London. By 2009 it did.

Second, the crash made an awful lot of people re-evaluate
what they wanted to do with their lives. Many London
craft breweries that set up between 2008 and 2011 were
founded by disillusioned people who used to work in
finance and IT, who wanted to so something more tangible
and meaningful. And third, more generally, people who
hated how large corporations had screwed the world
increasingly decided they wanted to by small and local,
and stick it to the big guy. The growing number of craft
brewers had a new audience that stretched well beyond
beer geeks.

By 2013, even your mum had heard of craft beer. BrewDog's antics gained mainstream media attention that then stayed with the beers and the people after the stunts had faded. Craft beer became a natural fit in a culture that was less about excess, more about moderation, premiumness, integrity and flavour.

Britain now has between three and four times as many brewers as it had at the turn of the Millennium. Craft beer is in every good bar and an increasing number of mainstream pubs, as well as the new craft beer bars that have sprung up in cities. A quarter of British adults claim to drink craft beer (even if they can't quite tell you what it is, exactly) and they have more styles and flavours to choose form than we've ever had before.

Craft beer is not an American phenomenon, but a global one. America was its catalyst, but its roots are in great British beer styles. These have been adapted and modernised, and enhanced by hops grown in the Pacific North West, Australia and New Zealand. Denmark is widely acknowledged as one of the most interesting places for craft beer in the world, while countries as diverse as Spain, Brazil and Japan are rapidly making their names as centres of brewing excellence.

Craft has revived brewing in traditional beer countries where it was flagging, and introduced quality, flavourful beer in countries that have never really considered it before. And the whole movement is global, constantly cross-fertilising and sharing.

Beer has changed forever. And there's never been a better time to drink it.

How beer is made

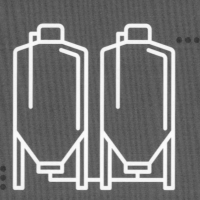

With a bunch of mysterious ingredients, a succession of shiny but impenetrable vessels, and an archaic set of terminology, the brewing process doesn't lend itself to easy explanation. But once you get it, you'll understand so much more about why beer is so special.

Beer is both extraordinarily simple and bewilderingly complex. We worked out how to make it 10,000 years ago, and yet we're still only just figuring out how it works. It's the most popular alcoholic beverage in the world, yet few of its drinkers can name its ingredients. We often think of beer as an everyday, ordinary beverage, but the processes that create it still seem miraculous to those who study them.

Beer books and craft beer bars everywhere can't wait to show a diagram of the brewing process, with its succession of shiny vessels. But before we get to that, what's beer made of anyway? Understand the ingredients and why they're there, and the process makes much more sense.

1. *The Ingredients of Beer*

Alcoholic drinks are created by the fermentation of sugar into alcohol. Mostly, those sugars occur naturally, and fermentation is itself a natural process that happens everywhere, without human help.

Generally speaking, when humans make booze, if the natural sugars come from fruit it's wine, and if those sugars come from grain, it's beer. So cider, often compared to beer, is actually a kind of apple wine, while sake, usually thought of as rice wine, is technically rice beer. All clear? Good.

At its simplest and oldest, beer is made by immersing sprouted grains in water, adding some sort of herbs or other plants for flavouring, and allowing yeast to ferment the sugar from the grain into alcohol. Simple eh? Today's beer ingredients are those that have been found to work best in this recipe, after thousands of years of trial and error.

Malted Barley

Beer can be made from any of the 'noble grains' we refer to as cereals, but by far the most common grain used is barley. This is the basic building block of beer, the equivalent of grapes in wine or apples in cider.

Before barley can be used for brewing, it needs to undergo a process of controlled sprouting and germination followed

by careful drying, which is known as malting. As well as providing that all-important fermentable sugar, malted barley provides a lot of the flavour and is usually the main influence on the beer's colour, and this is determined by the malting process.

Biologically speaking, fruits and grains both consist of seeds or embryos surrounded by a sugary stash of food to keep them alive until they can grow leaves and roots and feed themselves. When fruit ripens and rots, humans, animals and insects can attack it and claim the food for themselves. But grain is cleverer: it stores the embryo's sugar as long-chain starch molecules, which other organisms can't digest, and protects them with a rock-hard shell that animals can't penetrate. When the seed is ready to sprout, it releases enzymes that break down the starches into simpler, digestible sugars, and the seed wall softens so rootlets can sprout.

So before barley is used for brewing, the maltster tricks the seed embryo into thinking it's time to sprout, causing it to release its enzymes ready for conversion. With its job done, the maltster then kills the seed embryo by heating it, drying the malted barley until the brewer needs it.

This biochemistry stuff is fundamental to us being able to brew alcoholic beverages from grain; you can't get alcohol without the enzyme action. It's complicated – scientists only figured out what enzymes are less than 200 years ago – and yet humans knew the basic process as much as 10,000 years ago.

As well as enabling the enzyme activity, the drying process also dictates the flavours and colour in beer. Think of toast – another product of grains – and the range of colours you get as the bread turns from white to, if you leave it long enough, black. But as the colour changes, so does the taste, from light and crispy, through more savoury, to burnt.

Exactly the same thing happens with grain. Different reactions create different flavour properties, so maltsters use the drying process, playing with temperature, time and air circulation in the malting kilns, to create many different types of malt from the same barley grain.

The trouble is, if you heat the grain too far, you kill the enzymes and sometimes even caramelise the sugars. These grains may add wonderful flavours to beer, but they're no longer any good for getting what brewers refer to as 'fermentable extract', the sugars we want to turn into alcohol. That's why most beers that are darker than pale ale or lager use a cocktail of different malts.

MALT CHARACTER CHART

Example Malt	Typical Flavour characteristics	Example beer style
Pale Malt	Digestive biscuit	Lager, Pale ale
Crystal Malt	Granola Bar	IPA
Brown Malt	Nuttiness	Bitter
Dark Malt	Red Fruit, Chocolate	Porter
Roasted Barley	Coffee, Tobacco	Stout

This chart shows just a handful of the many different styles of malt available to brewers, some of their flavour characteristics, and an example of the style of beer you might expect to see this malt in. But even the darkest porter or stout will consist of around 90 per cent pale malt to provide the extract, with ten per cent darker grains to provide flavour, body and character.

Water

The biggest ingredient in beer is the one most people struggle to name. A finished beer is around 90-94 per cent water, and the water is doing much more than just making the rest of the ingredients runny.

Water isn't just water: it contains mineral ions and other deposits, and its pH is also a big influence on the enzyme activity of the malt and the overall character of the beer.

But the most important aspect of water for a brewer is its mineral content. This varies widely depending on where water is drawn from, and what kind of terrain it has seeped through to get there. Soft water has a very low mineral content, while in hard water it's very high.

Low mineral content suits styles such as pilsner lager, in which high mineral content would, among other things, make the hops taste too astringent.

Mineral-rich water, especially water high in sulphates, is perfect for India Pale Ale (IPA) because it gives a drier flavour and works well with the hops to enhance their bitterness.

It's no coincidence that the town of Plzeň in the Czech Republic, where pilsner lager was born, just happens to have water with negligible levels of mineral content, whereas Burton on Trent, where IPA was perfected as a style, has very high levels of sulphates in its wells. Beer styles evolve to suit the water deposits around them.

Hops

Hops are the superstar ingredient of beer. They're the only ingredient most people can name, the one that beer geeks even get tattoos of. People think of beer as being 'made from' hops, but it's more accurate to think of hops as the seasoning in beer. They're the equivalent of the herbs and spices that can turn a pan of chicken, garlic and onions in tomato sauce into either a Vindaloo or a Provençal stew.

Hops belong to the same family as the cannabis plant and the stinging nettle. Their flowers – or cones – are scaly and pale green, and contain high amounts of two

substances precious to brewers: alpha acids, and essential oils.

Alpha acids

These are the source of the bitterness in beer, which gives a nice balance and structure to the character of the malt, which could be sweet and sickly or one-dimensional without it. These acids also have an anti-bacterial effect, helping beer store for longer. Despite the popularity of pronounced hop flavours now, this anti-bacterial effect is almost certainly the reason hops became the dominant flavouring in beer.

Essential oils

A process called gas chromatography has detected over 400 different aroma compounds in hops, deriving from their essential oils. These compounds are also found in other plants, but the hop is unique in having such a high number of them in one place. These compounds can evoke flavours of tropical fruit, earthiness, spiciness, pine resin, flowers, freshly mown hay, and a whole host of other characteristics. The concentration of these different compounds varies depending on where the hops are grown, which means North American hops, Kentish hops and German hops all have quite different characteristics.

Until a few decades ago, most brewers were interested in hops only for their bitterness-giving properties. But the American craft beer revolution has spurred a global fascination with hop aromatics. The choice of hops – and the volume in which they are used – is the main attraction for many people coming to craft beer for the first time.

Yeast

Brewing yeast is a microscopic organism that eats sugar and excretes alcohol and carbon dioxide. It does this naturally to fruit where the skin is bruised or broken, and it does it to grain steeping in water after enzymes have converted starch to sugar. Brewing yeast – known as *Saccharomyces Cerevisiae* – is also the yeast that ferments bread, the alcohol burning off in the baking process while the CO_2 makes the bread rise. In fermentation, the CO_2 gives beer a natural sparkle, and the alcohol is of course preserved.

There are many different species of yeast. They evolve rapidly and cross-fertilise and, as well as creating alcohol, they can also add a wide range of flavour attributes, some pleasant to the human palate, others less so. Some yeast strains, as well as other bacteria that also ferment, can create distinct off-flavours that ruin the character the brewer is trying to create in the beer, so most brewers now isolate a single-strain yeast and propagate it in laboratory conditions. Many of these yeasts may have evolved over time to suit the brewery environment they live in, but with a few exceptions that evolution is now halted, so a brewer can create the same beer time after time.

The work to isolate and cultivate yeast strains was pioneered by Louis Pasteur and Emil Hansen, a scientist at the Carlsberg Laboratory. Hansen highlighted a single strain of yeast which he named *Saccharomyces Carlsbergensis* (later renamed *Saccharomyces Pastorianus*) and Carlsberg gave this technology to the brewing world, establishing precise distinctions between different types of yeast that had always been there, but were now completely controllable. It's the differences between these yeast types that create the main differences between styles of beer:

- Top-fermenting yeasts: prefer to ferment at slightly warmer temperatures, ferment quickly and leave some residual sugar in the beer, before rising to the top of the brew when they finish. These yeasts are used to brew ales.
- Bottom fermenting yeasts: prefer to ferment at cooler temperatures and take longer, but eat more of the fermentable sugar, leaving a crisper, cleaner beer, before sinking to the bottom of the brewing vessel. These yeasts are used to brew lagers.
- 'Wild' yeasts: more complex cultures that can occur naturally in the environment, used to brew Belgian lambic beers. These beers are often referred to as 'sours', but the yeast's contribution is more complex than that, adding earthy, spicy characteristics as well

as sharpness. While these yeasts are commonly thought of as wild, the most widely used ones, such as members of the Brettanomyces family, are now cultured just like other yeasts.
• Wheat beer yeasts: a family of top-fermenting ale yeasts that enjoy fermenting wheat sugars over barley, and create distinctive bugglegum, toffee or banana flavours in the finished beer.

... And anything else!

The modern version of the *Reinheitsgebot*, the German beer purity law first drafted in 1516, states that beer should only be brewed with hops, barley, yeast and water. Arguments about the wisdom or validity of this law still rage, but the vast majority of beers around the world are still made with these four core ingredients, and that's unlikely to change any time soon.

But craft brewers are nothing if not experimental. Brewers are now adding fruit, herbs and spices to the mix, which takes beer back to its origins, before hops became the dominant seasoning, and when the addition of fruit helped get the fermentation started. Today the addition of other ingredients is all about flavour and brewers are racing to push it as far as they can, in every direction they can. Be prepared for some experiments that will go disastrously wrong – that's what experimentation is all about – but someone is creating a new classic with the addition of hibiscus, pink peppercorns, coffee grounds or chilli even as you read this.

2. The Process

1. Mashing
2. Boiling
3. Fermentation
4. Conditioning
5. Ageing
6. Packaging

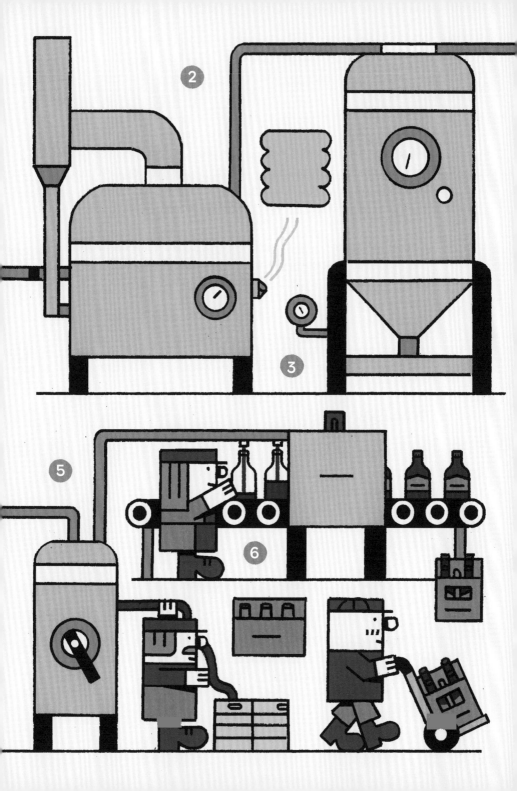

So now we know what goes into beer, it's time to confront the famous diagram of the succession of vessels. I've never thought of this as a particularly exciting or interesting way of helping people understand or appreciate beer, but the simple fact is that this is how beer is made and there's no getting away from it.

The thing is, once you understand the ingredients and why they're there, if you understand what's happening in each vessel and why, you can see what a miraculous process brewing really is.

1. Mashing
What Happens?
The malted barley has to be lightly crushed – not too much or it turns into flour, but enough for the grains to be broken and their contents able to be mixed. Some brewers buy their grain pre-milled, others mill it fresh on the premises (a choice similar to the one many households make with coffee beans).

Once crushed, the grain is mixed with water as it goes into the mash tun. The water is hot, but not boiling, and the brewer is aiming usually for a mashing temperature of between 62 and 65 degrees Celsius. The grain is stirred either manually or by mechanical panels in the tank to ensure a good, even mix.

Once it's stirred in, the grain will steep – or 'mash' – for about an hour before the resulting liquid is drained off, leaving the wet husks behind, to be recycled as animal feed. As the liquid is drained, more hot water is sprayed on top, to rinse out any remaining sugary deposits from the grain.

Why?
Malting began the activation process whereby the enzymes turn the grain's starch into simpler sugars, but the enzymes didn't complete that conversion. Now, sitting in an environment they're happy with, the enzymes break down starch into sugar, which dissolves in the water to give us a hot, sweet, sugary liquid known as wort. This is now the base of the finished beer.

2. Boiling
What Happens?
The sweet wort is filtered until it is clear, and then transferred to a vessel normally known as the copper, where it's heated to boiling for another hour or so. This is the stage at which the hops are added. Traditionally, there's one hop addition at the beginning of the boil, and another a few minutes from the end, or even after the burners beneath the copper have been turned off.

Why?
We want the hops to give two quite different characteristics to the beer: bitterness, and aroma (which is itself a big part of flavour). Boiling forces the hops through a process called isomerization, which turns their alpha

acids into iso-alpha acids. These are the source of hops' bitterness and their anti-bacterial properties. A good long boil maximises the bitterness available from the hops.

The problem is, this boiling also causes the precious, aromatic essential oils in the hops to flash off and evaporate. So more hops are added at the end of the boil, when their exposure to heat is not enough for them to lose their essential oils.

Brewers often use different varieties of hop at each stage, because those with high alpha acid content, which are more efficient at adding bitterness, aren't always the same varieties that give the desired aromas in the finished beer. Brewers therefore refer to bittering hops and aroma hops. Bittering hops tend to be cheaper and produced in bulk, while aroma hops are much more varied, with the most fashionable varieties often being very scarce.

3. Fermentation

What Happens?

The hopped wort goes through a heat exchanger that cools it from boiling to – usually – around twenty degrees Celcius, on its way from the copper to the fermentation vessel. Yeast is added, usually in the form of slurry, and the liquid sits at carefully controlled temperatures, usually for four or five days.

Why?

This is where the real magic happens. The yeast finds

itself in a rich, sugary environment, and goes on a frenzy of eating and reproduction, growing many times in mass, munching all the sugar and excreting alcohol and carbon dioxide, as well as flavour compounds.

Fermenting vessels vary in design depending on the whims of the chosen yeast — different yeasts like different conditions. Traditional pilsner brewers insist yeast favours horizontal tanks, which place less stress on it, but most commercial brewers use tall, conical fermenters, which are a far more efficient use of space and allow spent lager yeasts to be collected easily from the cone at the bottom. Some traditional ale brewers still use open square fermenters.

Any conscientious brewer chooses their style of fermenter based on one main criterion: keeping the yeast happy. Yeast is a living, temperamental creature, and if its surroundings and the ambient temperature are not to its liking, it may ferment poorly or even not at all, or may produce unpleasant off-flavours.

4. Conditioning

What Happens?
Once primary fermentation has ended, the beer is transferred to conditioning tanks for days or even weeks.

Why?
The yeast has done most of its work, consuming most of the fermentable sugars, and much of it is now dormant.

But there's still some activity going on. In the early stages, yeast throws out different alcohols, not all of them pleasant for human consumption. It also produces a wide variety of flavour compounds, some desirable, others not. In conditioning, or secondary fermentation, with the easy sugars gone the yeast reabsorbs some of these alcohols and flavour compounds, leaving a cleaner, smoother beer. This process is much longer for lager than for most ales, and should ideally be around four weeks. The word 'lager' derives from the German verb 'to store', and this is why.

5. (Sometimes) Ageing
What Happens?
Some beers may be transferred to a different vessel – usually wooden barrels – to age for up to a year or even longer.

Why?
Once conditioning has finished, most beers are best drunk as fresh as possible. The longer they age, the more likely some flavour compounds, particularly those contributed by the hops, will break down, and eventually the beer will taste stale and dull.

But in some beer styles, the flavours that develop with age can be interesting, and the ageing process itself can add new flavours from outside the brew. Depending on the age of a wooden barrel and what it's been used for before, an ageing beer can take on flavour from the wood itself, from the previous occupant of the wood (often whisky or wine) and from microorganisms living in the fibres of the wood, as well as other ingredients such as fruit or spices that may be added to the barrel.

Beer was stored in wooden barrels for most of its history. The likely contribution of flavour from barrels historically is hotly debated, but what's certain is that brewers today are ageing in wood quite specifically to develop new characteristics in the beer. The results may be inconsistent, because each barrel creates a slightly different microclimate for the beer, so barrels will be blended to achieve a pleasing whole.

6. Packaging
What Happens?
Normally, mainstream beer is filtered and/or pasteurised. It may be spun through a whirlpool instead of being filtered, and an increasing number of craft brewers leave their beer unfiltered and unpasteurised. Either way, the beer is then packaged in casks or kegs to be served on tap, or bottles or cans to be bought directly by the thirsty drinker.

Why?
Pasteurisation and filtration improve the stability and longevity of the beer, and filtration also helps greatly with its clarity. But these processes can also remove some of the flavour from the beer, so some craft brewers leave their beers unfiltered and unpasteurised, accepting that this

probably means a shorter shelf life for the beer. Casks are used for real ale, which is unfiltered and unpasteurised and still contains live yeast, which undergoes a secondary fermentation while it's in the pub cellar, creating greater complexity of flavour and a natural sparkle. Traditional kegs are pressurised and the beer – which has usually been pasteurised – is served with the addition of gas to give it its characteristic fizz. New innovations such as 'KeyKegs' blur the lines between these two mainstream formats, allowing unfiltered, unpasteurised beer to be served under pressure (so the beer pours freely without the need for the traditional real ale handpump).

Any beer packaging format is chiefly about protecting the beer. While drinkers regularly express a preference for clear glass bottles, these allow the beer to be 'sunstruck,' which makes it age rapidly. Green glass is better, brown glass is better still – the darker the glass, the more the brewer cares about beer quality over aesthetics.

Until very recently, cans were seen as inferior to bottles. Beer from cans gained a metallic tang, but new lining technology for cans has now removed this. The can protects the beer from sunlight completely. It's lighter and more recyclable, and for creative designers, the full surface of the can provides a much bigger canvas than the bottle label. For all these reasons, cans are now a resurgent format.

Beer styles

There's much more to beer than lager (and IPA. And stout.) But where do you start in trying to classify beers? And is it a good idea to try?

Oh boy, this is a thorny topic.

There are lots of people who are into beer who enjoy things being very neatly defined and precise. There are lots of others who see beer as fluid, metaphorically as well as literally; something that's constantly evolving. The concept of beer styles is where these two sides join in battle.

The late Michael Jackson was the first beer writer to attempt to categorise beer into a set of styles. It was a revolutionary move and did much to promote the understanding and appreciation of beer. He divided beers by the method of their fermentation, into top-fermenting and bottom-fermenting, and then sub-divided these into a total of 24 different styles.

Today, the American Brewer's Association lists a total of 152 different beer styles globally, and is constantly revising and updating its style guidelines.

So are there two styles of beer, or 24, or 152, or more?

When even the most rigorous systems of classification are regularly updated, this proves that beer styles evolve over time. Take IPA, for instance. It's common for beer geeks today to scoff at a beer such as Greene King IPA and say, "How dare they call that beer an IPA? It's only 3.4% ABV and it doesn't have any American hops!"

Well, IPA originally evolved in London, from a strong beer that was brewed to age for years. Lots of hops were added to preserve it, but hop character erodes over time, so the beer wouldn't have tasted particularly hoppy when it was finally drunk. We know from contemporary accounts that when brewers in Burton upon Trent began to brew IPA in the 1820s, its character changed dramatically from its London forebears. In the late nineteenth century the ABV fell dramatically thanks to changes in the way duty was calculated, so by the mid-twentieth century, pretty much any IPA you could find would have been similar in style to modern-day Greene King IPA. American craft brewers revived a more Victorian-style IPA in terms of strength and hop character, but the flavours we now love in American-style IPA would have been considered 'green' and 'unripe' in the days of the Raj. As late as the 1960s, the character of American hops was considered completely unsuitable for IPA and pale ales. Now American-style IPA is dominant across the world, and has given birth to black IPA, white IPA, session IPA, double IPA... there are even brewers experimenting with beer and cider hybrids some are calling 'apple IPAs'! Come back in thirty years, and IPA will mean something different again.

Well, it depends on how far you want to sub-divide. But however far you want to go, it makes sense to start with broad categories, and that's as far as we'll go here.

The main categories are defined chiefly by the type of yeast that ferments the beer. Then, we sub-divide mainly by colour, which is chiefly driven by the types of malt used. This creates some odd bedfellows, and if you cut it a different way, some beers would end up in different groups. But that's the fun of it.

Lagers

The definition of lager can be tricky, as there are two separate definitions that should go together, but don't always.

Let's start with the meaning of the word itself. Lager is German for 'store', and lager got its name because, if it's being brewed properly, it should be conditioned for several weeks at low temperatures. This helps the flavour stabilise and develop, and gives a true lager a subtle but naggingly insistent moreishness.

'Lagering' originated in the caves and deep cellars of what are now Germany and the Czech Republic – famous brewing towns such as Pilsen, Zatec and Freising are built on hills that are honeycombed with cool cellars.

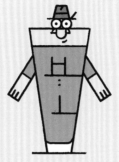

Four weeks is usually considered an appropriate period for lagering. For many commercial brands, this period has been reduced to just a couple of days, so by this definition, many of the biggest-selling 'lagers' in the world aren't technically lagers at all.

But there is another, entirely separate definition, and that's to do with the character of the yeast. Ales and lagers are fermented by different strains of yeast that have different characteristics and give different attributes to the beers. Lager yeasts tend to fall to the bottom of the brewing vessel after their long, slow fermentation, and are known as 'bottom fermenting' yeasts, while ale yeasts ferment quicker, rise to the top and are known as 'top fermenting' yeasts. Lager yeasts tend to eat more of the sugars and leave a thinner, crisper body and taste, while ales yeasts leave a little more body, and contribute fruity notes known as esters to the flavour of the beer.

Pale lagers

The style that dominates the world. In 1842 a brewery in Pilsen, in what is now the Czech Republic, combined pale malting technology with local water and ingredients, and German brewing know-how to create Pilsner Urquell. Most golden lagers today are pale imitations of it, tasteless and manufactured with an eye on cost savings over flavour. But this much-maligned style, which accounts for over 90% of the world's beer, can be as good as any other beer style when made with integrity and love.

POPULAR SUB-CATEGORIES: Pilsner, Helles
GREAT EXAMPLES: Pilsner Urquell, Camden Helles

Amber lagers

Before Pilsner's success German and Austrian brewers had perfected lagers that were deeper and richer but still crisp and refreshing. They never went away in Germany, and are enjoying a revival around the rest of the world.

POPULAR SUB-CATEGORIES: Bock, Märzen, Vienna Lager
GREAT EXAMPLES: Brooklyn lager, Paulaner Oktoberfest

Dark lagers

Lager isn't determined by its colour, and while it may be synonymous with the ubiquitous pale gold global suds, it can go as dark as any other beer. The combination of rich, roast flavours from dark malts and crisp finish and light body contributed by lager yeast isn't for everyone, but it's definitely worth exploring.

POPULAR SUB-CATEGORIES: Rauchbier (smoked beer), Schwarzbier (black beer), Munich Dunkel (Dark)
GREAT EXAMPLES: Schlenkerla, Asahi Black, Bernard Cerne

Ales

Ales may contribute less than ten per cent to the total volume of beer drunk in the world, but they make up the vast majority of different beer styles. Top-fermenting ale yeast was the original brewing yeast (lager yeast – a hybrid of ale yeast and a mysterious wild yeast – has so far been traced back to around the 14th century). Over millennia, ale has mutated in different parts of the world to inspire seemingly endless beer varieties.

Pale ales

What is 'pale'? Well, it's relative. It can be as golden as lager, or slightly darker, and to be honest, some resolutely 'pale' ales can actually be amber if you're going to be accurate about it. Pale ales are driving the current craft

beer boom, with a light malt character leaving the stage open to showcase the rich variety of hop characteristics available from around the world.

POPULAR SUB-CATEGORIES: English golden ale, American pale ale, India Pale Ale (IPA), some English best bitters and standard/ordinary bitters, Belgian blonde ales

GREAT EXAMPLES: Sierra Nevada Pale Ale, Thornbridge Jaipur, Brew Dog Punk IPA, Hopback Summer Lightning, Duvel

Amber ales

Bronze or caramel in colour, more likely to have chewier caramel or red fruit notes as well as decent hop character, the wonder of these beers is often in the perfect balance of their different component parts. Some 'red ales' are brewed with a hit of rye in the grain mix, which provides a drier astringency.

POPULAR SUB-CATEGORIES: some English best bitters and standard/ordinary bitters, American-style amber ale, Irish-style red ale, French bière de garde

GREAT EXAMPLES: Fuller's London Pride, Siren Liquid Mistress, BrewDog 5AM Saint

Brown ales

The classic rounded, nutty, mellow, autumnal style often dismissed by craft beer geeks as 'boring brown beer' is anything but if it's made and – just as importantly – kept with love and care.

POPULAR SUB-CATEGORIES: some English best bitters and standard/ordinary bitters, Scottish-style 'heavy' or 80/-, Extra Special Bitter (ESB)
GREAT EXAMPLES: Fuller's ESB, Five Points Brick Field Brown

Dark ales

More dark malts in the mix contribute rich, deep fruit, caramel, chocolate or chicory characteristics. There tends to be a lot more sweetness than in pale ale, which may or may not be balanced out by the hops, and can often be stronger in alcohol than other ales, though not always.

POPULAR SUB-CATEGORIES: Mild, old ale, barley wine, Scottish-style wee heavy, Belgian Dubbel
GREAT EXAMPLES: Mighty Oak Oscar Wilde Mild, Sierra Nevada Bigfoot, Westmalle Dubbel

Porters and stouts

Anyone who claims they know the difference between porter and stout is lying, it changes depending on where you go, what the history of styles was there, and who you ask. Both are dark, almost black looking, but redder if you hold them up to the light. They look forbidding and hard to drink, but standard versions are often much easier to get

on with than they seem. Having said that, this is the most popular style for barrel ageing, so at the top end, these can be the biggest, most complex, wine-like beers you'll find.

POPULAR SUB-CATEGORIES: Milk Stout, Smoked Porter, Russian Imperial Stout
GREAT EXAMPLES: Left Hand Milk Stout Nitro, Farmageddon Baltic Porter, Beavertown Smog Rocket, Goose Island Bourbon County

Wild and mixed fermentation beers

Since the 1880s, most commercial breweries have used yeasts that have been isolated and cultivated in laboratories. But yeast is everywhere, looking for sugar to ferment. It lurks in the fibres of wooden barrels, in rafters of old breweries, and on dust motes in the air. Yeast evolves and adapts to its climate and location, and there's been a revival of interest in brewing with 'wild' yeast cultures that inoculate the wort naturally.

This tradition almost died out in the twentieth century, because the results can be unpredictable and the flavours challenging. Often inaccurately and inadequately referred to as 'sour beers', these ales take tartness and many other characteristics from their mysterious outlaw yeasts, and from other microorganisms too. Sometimes beers undergo a 'mixed fermentation', being brewed initially with conventional yeast before being aged in wood where they take on an added layer of complexity.

Lambic and geuze

The Payottenland region on the outskirts of Brussels is the centre of the world when it comes to wild or spontaneous fermented beers. This is where a brewing method dating back to the sixteenth century survived the march of science. Lambic beers are inoculated by wild yeast as they sit in a broad, shallow vessel known as a coolship, and then aged in wooden barrels. Young lambics are sharp and loud, but they mellow over time and grow more complex. Lambics are not just sour: they exist on a scale that runs from tart and acidic through to austerely dry and musty, sometimes with eggy, cheesy or teenage bedroom notes,

but in a nice way. Because they can be unpredictable, they're often blended – usually young and old lambics together – to create geuze, which can still be a shock to your system if your new to it, but ultimately reveals itself as beer's answer to champagne.

POPULAR SUB-CATEGORIES: Kriek (with added cherries), Framboise (with added raspberries)
GREAT EXAMPLES: Cantillon Rosé de Gambrinus, Tilquin Geuze, Boon Kriek, Drei Fonteinen Oude Geuze

Flemish Red/Brown beers

In the nineteenth century, Belgian brewers such as Rodenbach took the basic principle of British porter brewing and played with it. Porter was aged in oak vats for up to a year, and the historical consensus is that a style we now associate with dark chocolate, coffee and red berry fruit flavours once had a sharp, spicy edge. *Brettanomyces*, the wild yeast characteristic of Belgian barrel-aged wild fermentation beers, was originally discovered in British ale casks and is Latin for 'British fungus'. British porter brewers were among the first to apply microbiology to

cleaning up their beers, but the Belgians took it the other way, brewing dark ales conventionally but then ageing them in wooden vats until they developed a distinctly tart character.

GREAT EXAMPLES: Rodenbach Grand Cru, Duchesse de Bourgogne

Saison

Not as dramatically wild as geuze or lambic, saison is supposedly the beer of the Belgian countryside, where light, refreshing beers were brewed for farmworkers. Saison yeasts have a funkier character than mainstream, cultured yeasts, but tend t give beer a spicy, earthy dryness rather than sourness.

GREAT EXAMPLES: Saison Dupont, Burning Sky Saison à la Provision

Kettle-soured beers

Yeast isn't the only organism to ferment in beer. Other microorganisms, chiefly lactobacillus, a lactic acid bacterium, is common to kimchi, sourdough bread and pickles, and can be used to create tart, acidic beers. A decade ago the only example of this style was Berliner Weisse, a low-strength sour wheat beer that was often drunk with fruit syrup shots at street kiosks in Germany. But the style is now enjoying a huge boost in popularity because it's a much easier, quicker and safer method of creating sour beer than lambic brewing. The lactobacillus

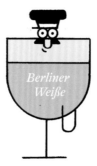

is introduced to the mash in the kettle, and the beer gets its sour character there before being fermented with a normal ale yeast. This is great for brewers who produce a wide portfolio of beers, because the alternative is to introduce a sour beer yeast to your fermentation vessels. Once it's there, if you're unlucky, the rest of your beers may end up sour whether you want them to or not. So if you have a sour beer from a new craft brewer, chances are it's a riff on this style.

GREAT EXAMPLES: The Kernel London Sour, Siren Calypso

Wheat beers

Over thousands of years, barley has emerged as the best grain for brewing beer. But beer can be brewed with other cereals too, such as oats and rice. Wheat beers make it into a category of their own because while they're strictly speaking top-fermenting beers, there are different strains of yeast that prefer fermenting wheat over barley, and those yeasts throw off some very particular flavour compounds, creating banana, spice or bubblegum aromas.

The two great wheat beer traditions belong to Bavaria and Belgium. The Belgians tend to add flavourings such as coriander, curaçao and orange peel to create zesty, vibrant beers, whereas the Germans keep it pure and allow the complex flavours created by the yeasts and the wheat to shine through.

Some brands and some bars will attempt to make you put pieces of fruit in your wheat beer. If these flavours were meant to be in there, the brewer would have added them, so you don't have to. It's your beer. You've paid for it. If you want to stick a fruit salad in there, away you go. But there is no truth to the idea that this is how these beers are 'supposed' to be served.

Cloudy wheat

Wheat beers are naturally hazy, an effect caused both by the proteins in the wheat and the presence of the yeast, which stays in suspension longer than in other beers. This haze can settle out in bottled beers, and some brewers suggest pouring the beer carefully so you have the option of tasting it clear, then swirling the last fifth of the bottle to agitate the yeast and pout it into the glass. If you do this, you'll notice the clear beer is crisper, while the liquid haze gives it more body and a fuller, rounder flavour.

POPULAR SUB-CATEGORIES: German Hefeweizen, Belgian witbier
GREAT EXAMPLES: Weihenstephaner Hefe Weissbier, St Bernardus Witbier

Crystal wheat

Like any other beer, wheat beer can be filtered so that it pours clear. Known as kristallweizen in Germany, you lose a lot of wheat beer's clove and banana character when you do this, but it still retains a zesty, refreshing character.

GREAT EXAMPLES: Schneider Weisse Kristall, Goose Island 312

Dark wheat

Wheat beers are usually a mix of wheat and barley malts. Traditionally, these beers like most beers were darker than they are now, and German Dunkelweizen get their deeper colour from the same malts that make Munich or Vienna-style lager, giving a wonderful rich, sweet, banoffee character.

GREAT EXAMPLES: Franziskaner Dunkel Hefe-Weisse

How to
taste beer

You've been drinking beer wrong your whole life! Actually, no, you haven't. You can drink however you like. But if you take your time over it, any good beer will reveal much more of itself to you.

Most of the time, when you're drinking beer you don't spend too much time thinking about what's going on in the mouth, and that's fine; beer is a social lubricant, and while you're drinking it, most of your attention is focused elsewhere.

But just like when you read half a page of a book and realise you haven't taken it in because you've been thinking about something else, or there's music playing and you can't recall what the last few songs were because you were listening to your friend talking, there's a big difference between sensory stimulus being picked up by your mouth, nose and eyes and your brain actually paying any attention.

If you've paid a few quid for your special craft beer, you may want to make sure you're getting your money's worth. That's why truly *tasting* beer is different and more involved than merely *drinking* it. So here are some guidelines to extracting the most from your beautiful beer.

Ambience

You know that time you went on holiday and loved
the local beer or wine and you brought a bottle home
and it tasted awful? You weren't just being daft: your
surroundings really do make a big difference to your
perception of flavour. Neuro-scientific research has shown
that the ambient noise, other smells in the room, the
people you're with, even the colour of the walls can all
make a difference. So make sure you're in a place where
you can really focus on the beer, where as much as possible
outside the glass is neutral. And talking of glass...

Glassware

If you drink straight from the bottle or can, you're cutting
your nose out of the equation and losing not just the
aromas, but a lot of the flavour. The best glasses are those
you can swirl and stick your nose in. There are plenty of
well-designed beer glasses around now, the 'teku' being
my own personal favourite for tasting because it has a nice
bowl to collect the aromas and it makes beer look great.
But if you haven't got access to anything else, use a good-
sized wineglass, leaving enough room in the glass for air to
circulate.

Temperature

You should drink beer at whatever temperature you prefer
it. But chances are, you normally drink it a couple of
degrees colder than the optimal temperature for tasting.
The colder a beer is, the more its flavours are masked:

as it warms, it opens up. Normal guidelines are that lager should be served between four and seven degrees Celsius, IPAs and pale ales a little warmer, around eight to 10 degrees, and darker real ales at 10 to 13 degrees. Personally I'd have porters, stouts and barley wines at room temperature, but the myth that traditional English beers should be served 'warm' dates back to when our average room temperature was around 10 degrees cooler than it is now.

Appearance

Beer judges usually give marks for clarity, but in an age of cloudy craft beers, this is problematic. Some truly revolting beers look bright and sparkling, while hazy beers can be bursting with fresh hop flavour. So the most important questions are: Does it look like you expected it to? Does it look like you want it to? Does it make you want to drink it?

Take a good sniff

This is where the sniffing and swirling are really important, getting oxygen into the beer and releasing its volatile flavour compounds. Dig your nose into the glass and breathe deeply. Too often, this bit turns into a contest as to who can highlight the most refined flavour notes:
"I'm getting marmalade."
"Yes, me too – Seville orange marmalade. From Waitrose."

This ultimately gets boring, and it's about point-scoring rather than truly enjoying the beer. Instead of thinking of

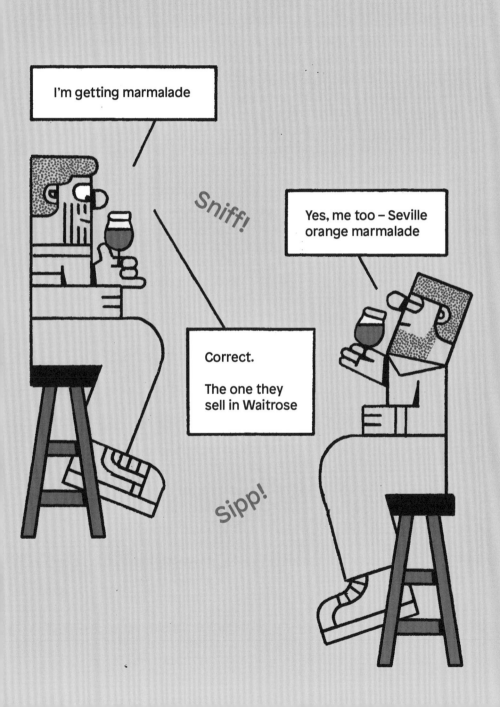

this stage as an identity parade of flavour notes, what if you think of it as a courtship? Is there any aroma at all? If not, why not? Aroma should entice you. Does it put you off instead? Or does it make you want to plunge in? With some great and powerful beers, the aroma makes you want to carry on sniffing, almost forgetting to drink. On a few rare occasions, as with fresh coffee or freshly baked bread, the delivery may not even live up to the aroma's promise. But overall, looking for aroma to increase the anticipation and desire of finally taking a drink. However it might do that, if it isn't doing it, it's not working.

Take a good swig

Obviously, this is the main event. In the first second in which the beer enters your mouth, there's an initial flash of flavour sensation, before your rational, analytical brain kicks in. Can you capture that and appreciate it? How does it make you feel? I'm increasingly of the opinion that to really get this, you should start by taking a generous swig rather than a dainty sip.

Keep it in your mouth. There are taste receptors all over your mouth, not just your tongue, so roll it around.

Once it develops, is there a journey across the palate? Does it develop as it moves around your mouth, or as it sits there, or is it just a quick flash of something that quickly disappears? Is it complex or one-dimensional?
If it's trying to be simple and direct and refreshing, does it do that job well or are there odd bits sticking out? If it's trying to be complex and rewarding, are all those

constituent parts that beer-spotters love identifying so much working together or do they jar with each other?

Swallow

Humans actually get most of our aroma sensations from 'retronasal olfaction,' meaning you really get it when it's in your mouth and when you're swallowing, and it passes up to your nasal cavity from the back of your throat, and past your olfactory bulb as you breathe out through your nose. But there's a broader sensory aspect to this, too. How do you feel once you've swallowed that first sip? Are you satisfied? Do you want to drink more?

This is revealing - how many times do you not feel this to be the case, but you force the beer down anyway, because you've paid for it? How many flabby beers do you finish with grim determination? And how many times does the finishing buzz compel you to raise the glass again, to try to complete a circle, to nag away at the desire the beer has created?

Repeat

If the beer is any good, you'll want to drink more. You've worked hard and extracted a great deal of what the beer has to offer, but often the character develops further the more you drink. When you feel satisfied that you've got to know the beer properly, you can start talking to the people you're with again. They're probably getting a little impatient with you by now. Time to switch back from tasting to drinking.

Great beer *countries* of the world

There's no tourism like beer tourism. See the world with beer as your guide, and you'll see it in a more open, friendlier and more interesting way than any tourist brochure or guidebook could tell you.

Wherever humans settle, they work out how to ferment the local vegetation into something alcoholic. It's probable that knowledge of brewing emerged independently in different places around the world, but as a general rule, agricultural land tends to split into temperate regions where grain (and hops) grow better than grapes, and warmer regions where grapes grow better than grain. So in recent history, northern European nations brewed beer, while their southern neighbours made wine. America, once colonised, had bits that suited both.

This distinction is breaking down now, thanks chiefly to the globalisation of trade, aided in a small but significant way by climate change. So while the great traditional brewing nations of the world naturally centre around northern Europe, interesting brewing cultures are emerging all across the world.

It's tempting to look at the great Trappist tradition of Belgium, the cask ales of Britain, German lagers and wheat beers and Czech pilsners, and talk about how each country went its own way, developing its unique beer styles independently, until the modern craft beer revolution mixed them all up in a wonderful melting pot of styles.

Tempting, but wrong.

These traditions and the technologies that support them have been cross-fertilising, inspiring and stealing from each other, for centuries. Without Flemish hops, we wouldn't have hoppy English IPAs. Without the pale malting technology developed by the early brewers of those IPAs, we wouldn't have golden lager. Without big golden lager brewers, we wouldn't have the understanding of yeast that every brewer around the world, large and small, now benefits from. But each brewing nation took the common pool of brewing technology and ingredients and developed them in quite different ways.

The UK

It's a peculiarly British trait that we find it difficult to celebrate anything we do well. All the biggest beer brands and breweries in the UK are foreign-owned and the lagers they produce originated elsewhere, even if they're now brewed under licence in the UK (and, of course, if they're brewed here, they obviously can't be as good as they are in their country of origin).

Even craft beer drinkers favour American hops and beer styles over their British equivalents, or celebrate the mysteries of Belgium's Trappist and lambic beers over home grown 'boring brown beer'.

But talk to the Americans who founded the first craft breweries and they'll tell you British ales were one of, if not the, main inspiration. Dig a little into the history of Belgian sour ale or strong Tripels, and you'll find a distinctively British influence there too. German and Austrian amber lagers were vastly improved after their brewers stole pale malt technology from Burton upon Trent. The man who founded Carlsberg sent his son – the eponymous Carl – to study in Burton. And when Louis Pasteur worked out the behaviour of yeast, he shared his discovery with London's porter brewers before anyone else.

Britain was the birthplace of the Industrial Revolution, the first country to urbanise, creating concentrated markets that allowed brewers to grow in scale. Technologies such as steam power, the hydrometer, the microscope and the introduction of railways helped the world's first industrial-scale brewers grow bigger than anyone had seen before. Porter and stout, IPA and pale ale – the styles that now dominate the global craft brewing scene – were all born in the British Isles, with porter and IPA both originating in London.

The British have always been enthusiastic drinkers, providing abundant demand for the beer these brewers produced. And an Empire that functioned on global trade meant these beers spread around the world – IPA was the first global beer style, and Bass the first global brand. Britain resisted the march towards interchangeable, globalised lager brands much longer than most other countries. Pilsner style lagers were ubiquitous globally by the early twentieth century, but it wasn't until the 1970s that the style really got off the ground here.

The Campaign for Real Ale (CAMRA), formed in 1971 to protect and preserve traditional British beer, led the

resistance to lagerisation. 'Real ale' consisted chiefly of bitter, pale ale and mild, with golden ales emerging later to lure lager drinkers back over. These were the beer styles in which the American craft beer revolution found its roots: darker, more flavourful, more traditional – they were as different from mainstream lager as you could get back in the 1970s and 1980s.

When the craft beer revolution came back across the Atlantic, Britain's small brewers dug deeper into the archives and revived porter and stout, barley wines and old ales. They also made a break with preserving a shrinking, narrowing tradition and embraced other styles from around the world. As we are in many things, Brits will always be in thrall to whatever is coming out of the US (British brewers now brew with more American hops than British hops) but Britain now has a more diverse array of beer styles – traditional, international and experimental – than it's ever had before.

The best place to enjoy beer in Britain is the pub, unrivalled anywhere outside the British Isles. Some might differentiate between traditional boozers and hip, new craft beer bars, but the pub has always evolved to suit its times, and this, along with tiny micropubs, is merely the next stage.

Country pubs are invariably more traditional and conservative, but wonderful for that, while craft beer tends to focus on cities, especially those with young student populations. Most people think of craft beer as a London thing, but it was well established in other cities before

London took control. Burton is more important to the history of beer than any other city save maybe Munich, and Sheffield has an insane number of beers available at any given time.

KEY STYLES: bitter, pale ale, IPA, stout, porter
KEY DESTINATIONS: London, Burton upon Trent, Sheffield, Norwich, Bristol

Germany

Where the UK and Belgium stand for ale and eclecticism, Germany, just as traditional, is all about lager and consistency. But that's by no means as dull and uniform as it might sound.

The modern history of German beer is dominated by a piece of legislation passed in Bavaria in 1516. The *Reinheitsgebot*, almost in passing in a document concerned chiefly with the pricing of beer, stated that beer could only be brewed with barley, hops and water (yeast, when it was discovered and understood, was added centuries later). The motives and wisdom behind the legislation have been hotly debated. But its influence on German brewing is unarguable for both its supporters and its bitter opponents.

It's likely that a leading motive behind the *Reinheitsgebot* was the preservation of a Bavarian beer identity. Of all German regions, Bavaria is fiercely proud of its beer, and the national adoption of the Reinheitsgebot was a condition of Bavaria joining a united Germany.

There's nothing in the *Reinheitsgebot* that prohibits the brewing of ale with these core ingredients, but at the time it was passed, Bavaria was brewing bottom-fermented lagers and ageing them in cool caves and cellars, and this is the style that eventually came to dominate German brewing. Curiously though, although there's seemingly a stylistic uniformity, Germany has never produced a large global brewing conglomerate; beer tastes in the country remain fiercely local, and Germany never experienced the dramatic consolidation in the number of brewers that the UK and US did.

German beer can be misleading from the outside. Exports all tend to be golden pilsners or Munich-style wheat beers (which were given a *Reinheitsgebot* exemption for the Bavarian princes who brewed them). Only when you travel across Germany do you see that lager can rival ale in its diversity.

Munich may be the first city tourists associate with beer thanks to Oktoberfest, the biggest beer festival in the world (although the locals think of it more as a celebration of Bavarian identity than beer itself). But head north on the train for two or three hours and you arrive in the stunning medieval town of Bamberg. For beer aficionados, this is Germany's capital.

Bamberg is chiefly famous as the home of rauchbier, in which the barley is smoked over beechwood during the malting process to give it an intense smoky flavour reminiscent of bacon. It's an acquired taste. But Bamberg is a beer town that's about the whole range of German styles. Its brewpubs offer strong Märzens, dark, rich bocks, and demonstrate clear differences between Helles and Pilsner, two pale golden styles that are often considered interchangeable.

All of these are lagers. All of them are excellent. It's curious that Germany, like every other country, is keen to adopt the global, IPA-led craft beer template when, if you look at it in the right way, Germany has had its own craft beer culture all along. It never lost the spirit of localism, craft and excellence that countries such as the UK and US are now trying to regain.

KEY STYLES: Pilsner, Helles, Bock, Märzen, Oktoberfest, Rauchbier, Weizen
KEY DESTINATIONS: Bamberg, Munich, Düsseldorf, Cologne, Berlin

Czech Republic

Famously, the Czechs are the biggest per capita beer drinkers in the world. Beer isn't just a drink there; it's part of being Czech.

A book could be written analysing the complex social, anthropological and political factors behind this, but one contributing factor is certainly the presence of Saaz hops, which just happen to be the finest lager brewing hops in the world. (If you fancy buying some direct, at the time of writing the waiting list means you should be firing up the copper some time after the 2022 harvest.)

Just down the road from the town of Saaz – or Žatec, to give the town and its hops their correct Czech name – is Pilsen (Plzeň). Here, in 1842, the brewing world pivoted on its axis.

Like all Czechs, the burghers of Plzeň were fiercely proud of their beer, and there was collective horror one day when the municipal brewery's beer was deemed so bad it had to be poured away. The Czechs hired a German brewer who combined Saaz hops with lager yeast, new pale malt and the incredibly soft water of the region to create Pilsner Urquell, or 'the original Pilsner'. Claims that this was the world's first golden lager are almost certainly untrue,

but the recipe and ingredients unarguably created a new beer style that, with the aid of refrigeration and railway transport, swept across Europe and then the world. Today, the vast majority of commercially available beers are pale imitations of Pilsner Urquell.

Other brewers in the Czech Republic rapidly reproduced the style, and while beer aficionados around the world refer to Pilsner, within the Czech Republic they don't always want to stand in thrall to the town. Light, golden lagers are more often referred to as *Svetly Lezak*, (literally, light/

pale lager). *Svetly* is an alluring beer, and it gives the lie to the notion that lager has to be tasteless and fizzy in order to be drinkable. *Svetly* has flavour. The hops are assertive, not in the obvious manner of an IPA, but gently nagging, balanced and bright and always bringing you back for more. Beer is relatively cheap ('The government that raises the price of beer shall fall', goes an old proverb). It's served liberally and joyfully, with a big, foaming head, and if you don't want a second, third or even fourth, the brewer will think they haven't done their job properly.

This is flavourful beer brewed to be drunk in large quantities. If flavourful beer was somehow challenging or difficult to drink, the Czechs wouldn't be the biggest beer drinkers in the world.

KEY STYLES: Pilsner lager
KEY DESTINATIONS: Prague, Pilsen, České Budějovice

Belgium
There are still people out there who labour under the illusion that Belgium is a boring country. These people have obviously never encountered Belgian beer.

As well as having the most interesting and eclectic set of beer styles in the world, Belgium is also the birthplace of surrealism. Get to know Belgium, and it seems clear that one influenced the other; it's just difficult to tell which is the chicken and which the egg.

When everyone else zigs, Belgium zags, and nowhere is

this truer than in beer. Before the industrial revolution, brewing happened on farms, in villages and in monasteries. When the great scientific innovations of the late nineteenth century transformed brewing, the Belgians quickly realised that big brewing companies with the capital to invest in new technology and large, concentrated urban markets to supply, would grow to become national and international concerns. They also realised that tiny, rural Belgium wouldn't be able to compete in this beery arms race. Led by the Trappist monasteries, who began brewing commercially in the late nineteenth century after having been destroyed by Napoleon Bonaparte, Belgium set off on a different path, keeping its beer styles eclectic and varied, embracing wild and mixed yeasts even as brewers such as Heineken and Carlsberg began brewing with single-strain, laboratory cultured yeasts that guaranteed each pint of beer would taste the same.

Most Belgian beer styles that are revered today began in the first few decades of the twentieth century. They feel like they should be much older, and certainly their roots are, but Trappist Dubbels and Tripels are only a century old in their current incarnation. Lambic and geuze go back to the sixteenth century, but were increasingly becoming a minority interest. Flemish brown beers were developed from English porters in the nineteenth century. Belgium quite deliberately developed a beer identity that was quite distinct from the progress towards international pilsner brands.

The First World War transformed beer, just as it did the rest of the country. Affection for the liberating British tommies meant English-style ales entered the big mix of Belgian styles. The global wave of prohibitionary measures on booze saw the alcohol content of beer severely restricted in the UK and outright prohibition in the US. The Belgian version was to ban spirits but not to regulate beer, so in response, Belgian brewers upped the ABV of their beers so that a Belgian blonde ale is typically 6% ABV, Dubbel 7-8% ABV and Tripel 8-9% ABV.

But Belgian drinkers, like their counterparts across the world, were increasingly drawn to Czech and German-

style pilsner. The locally brewed versions, Jupiler and Stella Artois, grew to dominate the market. By the 1970s, many brewers of Belgium's unique styles were growing old, facing dwindling markets and little enthusiasm from younger generations.

This changed when, quite by accident, beer writer Michael Jackson stumbled across Belgian beer. He fell in love instantly, and became a champion of Trappists, abbey beers, saisons and sours across the world. The export orders − particularly from the United States − revived an entire industry.

The best thing about a visit to Belgium today is that even the boring, bog-standard selection is extraordinary compared to any other country. Find a pavement café in any city, town or village and you'll have a choice of beers such as Duvel, Chimay, Westmalle Dubbel, Palm Speciale and Rodenbach. That's *normal*. The specialist bars will have beer lists running to the hundreds, with aged and rare variants you simply can't find anywhere else. Served impeccably in the correct branded glassware, accompanied by cheese and salami that is objectively awful but somehow irresistible, especially when dipped in mustard and celery seeds, the combination of Belgium's potent, mysterious and sometimes downright weird beers, and the deliciously laid-back, mellow bars that serve them, make this one of the best drinking experiences in the world.

And then, when you know a little more, and you start to track down the lambics of Cantillon and Boon, the wood-aged Flanders reds and the bottles of Orval that are saved

until well past their 'best before' dates and then sold
at a premium; when you finally track down a bottle of
Westvleteren 12 and compare it to Rochefort 10 or St
Bernardus Abt 12 and realise they're just as good at a
fraction of the price... well, then you're in love for life.
You may get lured away by the call of American hops for
a while, but whenever you find yourself at a dead end,
Belgium is always there to inspire you again. The best
beer destination in the world is only a Eurostar away.

KEY STYLES: Saison, Lambic, Geuze, Dubbel, Tripel, Flemish
Brown
KEY DESTINATIONS: Brussels, Ghent, Bruges

United States

Not so long ago, American beer was a joke – a poor joke,
that involved analogies with making love in a canoe.
But a period of just twenty years saw the US go from
the back of the pack in the race to brew interesting beer
to become the leader of a craft beer movement that has
gone global.

American beer wasn't always bad. The United States
once drank more cider than anything else, but in the
1870s talented German brewers left their home country
amid political turmoil, and made it to the US to find
seemingly limitless land on which to grow good barley
and hops. Adolphus Busch, Adolph Coors and Frederick
Miller – whose names would grow to dominate brewing
across the continent – all founded their breweries in
different parts of the country in this period.

But when the manufacture, sale and distribution of alcohol was prohibited by the Volstead Act of 1919, beer disappeared, or at least went underground. When prohibition was repealed in 1933, America had lost its taste for bitter beer. A generation had grown up on soft drinks, and beer had to be light, cold and sweet to satisfy them.

Miller, Coors and Anheuser Busch emerged as regional brewing powerhouses, and in the 1970s embarked on the

'beer wars' to destroy each other. Miller launched Miller Light with the tagline 'Everything you want in a beer, and less,' and another layer of flavour and character was stripped from American beer. When the smoke of the multi-million dollar marketing campaigns cleared, each of the Big Three was more powerful than ever – but they'd killed off hundreds of smaller American brewers. Soon, 80% of the entire beer market belonged to these three brewers of light beer that was almost indistinguishable from one brand to the next.

No one really paid much attention when Fritz Maytag, heir to the washing machine empire, started the Anchor Steam brewery in San Francisco in 1974. But five years later, when prohibition's last hangover – the ban on home brewing – was repealed, Maytag was seen as a prophet for the new wave of craft beer that would emerge. By the mid-1980s, small-scale American brewers were reviving, recreating and reinterpreting traditional beer styles from across the world.

America is a country of great vision. In one sense, it has to be BIG, with the ambitious reaching for a scale to match the landscape. In another, it's a nation that's always pushing at the frontier, trying to discover what's new. The big brewers achieved the scale, while the new generation of craft brewers would eventually push beer beyond any frontiers it had previously known.

Unlike every other country listed above, America had no precious brewing tradition left to preserve. It was new to begin with, and was snuffed out by prohibition within fifty years of really getting established. This left American craft brewers free to look forward. After they realised how the flavours of American hops could transform traditional European styles, they pushed hop character as far as it could go, with 'double' and 'Imperial' IPAs. When they became proficient in German, British and Belgian style beers, they began to combine elements of these styles.

The flavours in American craft beer were cleaner, more precise and often more dramatic than their European inspirations. And they tended to have more modern branding, a more open way of talking about brewing, style and flavour. In the past twenty years this approach has become a template for craft brewers around the world, with brewers everywhere trying to get their hands on American hops.

In America itself, the emphasis is on freshness and localism. Few of America's 5,000 beers have national distribution. Any beer bar will recommend drinking what's local. And keeping supply lines short – and chilled – is the best way to preserve the flavours of those wonderful hops. The best place to get American, or even American-style beer, is the US itself.

KEY STYLES: American IPA, pale ale, American light lager, Imperial Stout
KEY DESTINATIONS: Portland, Seattle, Denver, San Diego

And emerging ones to watch...

There are now craft breweries recorded in over 200 countries worldwide. You can find beers like BrewDog, Brooklyn and Sierra Nevada pretty much wherever you go. But here are some countries that are emerging on to the scene with new craft brewing traditions of their own.

Australia and New Zealand

Known for swilling tins of ice-cold lager over the stereotypical barbie, Australians increasingly give a XXXX for other beer styles. New Zealand began the charge with the discovery that hops grown in the Nelson region – home of Kiwi sauvignon blanc – had a character that rivalled that of hops grown in the American Pacific North West but was different from it, resembling that of the local wine. Tasmania then countered with Galaxy, a hop rich in passion fruit character that finds its perfect expression in fruity, light but flavourful pales as such as Stone & Wood's Pacific Ale, which is brewed to match Australia's hot, humid climate.

Brazil

With no real beer styles to call its own, Brazil is proving such a good mimic of American, German, British and

Belgian styles that in international competitions
the copies are now regularly beating the originals.
Countries across South America are watching with
interest and creating their own ideas, but beer quality
in Brazil has shown an incredible improvement over
the last decade.

Italy

Italian food and drink is all about local provenance.
There are nearly a thousand brewers in Italy now,
but there aren't many locally grown hops. So what
can they do? The answer is to explore beer's other,
overlooked ingredients. Italy grows a number of
interesting grains such as spelt and old wheat varieties,
and an increasing number of breweries are creating
beers that no longer follow Belgium, Germany or the
US as their predecessors did, but are unmistakeably
original and Italian.

Spain

Spain has always been a great place to drink beer, and
the quality of its lagers is often overlooked. (If you
doubt that, just try the local brand next to the British
imports served up to package holiday tourists.) But
now, small Spanish brewers are showing remarkable
levels of inventiveness and intuition to create beers
that blur traditional boundaries.

An *introduction* to home brew

Once something foul that sat in your weird uncle's airing cupboard, home brewed beer is now at the forefront of the craft beer revolution.

Governments are funny about allowing people to make their own booze. To paraphrase Bill Hicks: if you make a process that happens in nature illegal, aren't you saying that God made a mistake? But God wasn't thinking about tax revenue when she created fermentation. Home brew was effectively illegal in the UK from 1880 until 1963, and in the US from 1919 till 1979.

When home brew was legalised in 1963, British beer drinkers had one goal in mind: cheap beer. They weren't particularly interested in how you made it so long as it was alcoholic. Why go to all the trouble of understanding the delicate interplay of grain, yeast and spiky little flowers when you could just buy a kit of sugary syrups and powdered yeast from Boots and add water? During its first boom in the 1970s and 1980s, British home brewing was the alcoholic equivalent of the Pot Noodle. The only good thing enthusiasts had to say about their issue was that it only cost them 3p a pint. Their guests would silently fume that, at this price, they had been fleeced.

When they got their turn, the Americans approached brewing in a completely different way. They weren't as bothered about the cost as they were about brewing beer that tasted better than what was commercially available. While many of that first generation of home brewers went on to found the first wave of craft breweries, home brew became firmly established as a serious hobby.

Those with an engineering frame of mind built miniature versions of proper brewery set-ups in their garages. Initially, the vogue was to create 'clone brews' of famous beers, with people trying to 'scavenge' yeast from Belgian and British bottle-conditioned ales to use in a new brew.

Once they became proficient in the art of cover versions of great beers, some home brewers set out to create their own compositions. Brewing is simply cooking – many of us buy ready meals or fast food, then when we start cooking for ourselves we follow recipes religiously. If we do this enough, we start to develop an understanding of ingredients and processes, and develop the skill to adapt recipes or even create them.

Home brewing is no different. And just as you can buy books of recipes from your favourite celebrity chefs, so you can now find home brew books that tell you how to recreate your favourite beers, written by people like Sam Calagione, founder of Dogfish Head brewery, or Mitch Steele from Stone. Others have collected recipes from rock star brewers – and BrewDog have released all theirs online – so there's no shortage of inspiration.

But many home brewers graduate to writing their own recipes. On a small scale, they can experiment with different hop varieties and hopping rates, introduce quirky new ingredients to see if they work, change things around, and the stakes when things go wrong are relatively small.

This nimble approach means the committed home brewer – with the appropriate skill and high enough standards – can create beers that rival or even beat their commercial counterparts. This author has judged many home brew competitions and found that the general standard tends to be a little higher than competitions for small local commercial breweries. The commercial brewer simply takes a bottle, can, keg or cask off the regular line and sends it in, whereas the home brewer painstakingly practices and tweaks the recipe until they're happy with it. The list of no-shows at some competitions is testament to the fact that sometimes, the final brew simply isn't judged good enough by its creator.

The process of brewing is simple to understand, but requires focus and discipline if you're going to do it well. It takes time and experience to get to competition level. Whatever your ambition, it's probably best to start off simply and see how you go, as you learn more about the brewing process and gain confidence.

Starter Kits

The kind of thing you used to be able to buy in Boots is still around, albeit much better quality. The basic kit you need consists of a large plastic container – generally holding about 40 pints – plus essential equipment comprising a hydrometer (to measure fermentable sugar content, or 'gravity'), a thermometer, steriliser, bottles, caps and bottler.

The simplest possible form of brewing with this kit is to buy a concentrated syrup that combines wort and hop extract, and follow the instructions. All you do is dilute the syrup with hot water, then, when it reaches the right temperature, add the yeast, and then keep a close eye on fermentation. Don't get lazy or jump the gun – at any level of brewing, cleanliness is absolutely vital – any stray microorganisms can ruin the brew. And getting the temperature wrong can kill or harm the yeast.

Brewing with hop and malt extracts

Once you're confident with these steps, you can start playing with different kinds of malt and hop extracts instead of one pre-made syrup kit, and start to tweak and create your own recipes. This stage requires an additional piece of equipment: the vessel that brewers refer to a copper, where hops or hop extract is boiled.

Your initial copper could be a large saucepan until you're ready to invest in a more serious bit of kit. Once you're confident, you can start experimenting with whole leaf hops or hop pellets rather than pre-made hop extract.

Brewing with all- or part-grain

The final stage of transition to a version of what commercial brewers do is to mash your own wort instead of using malt extract. Here, you buy malted barley grains and infuse them in warm water ('mashing' them the same way you mash tea, to extract flavour compounds from plant matter.) You could in theory do this in your saucepan, but it's very difficult to do over a direct heat source: you're looking for a consistent warm temperature – let it get too hot and you risk killing the enzymes in the grain that convert starch to sugar. What you ideally need is an insulated vessel where you can add water and get the temperature right, then leave it for the mashing period. A popular way of doing this is to get a customised coolbox, with a wire mesh layer on the bottom to separate the spent grain from the wort, and a tap on the side to draw the wort off. Trading up from this, you can buy small, thermostatically controlled homebrew mash tuns.

With this level of equipment, you can still buy kits that exactly recreate your favourite beers – you're just buying the hops, yeast and grain as separate components. But you can also buy any other hops, yeast or grain that take your fancy from homebrew suppliers, and create your own recipes.

Some home brewers with an engineering bent take pride in building their own home breweries from basic household supplies, fitting thermometers, heating coils and thermostats to cool boxes, pans and plastic buckets. But you can spend £600 to £700 and get a state-of-the-art, custom-made home brewery.

Any expert home brewer would recommend starting with a simple kit — the recipe may be taken care of, but there's still a lot to learn about cleaning and temperature, monitoring fermentation, bottling in a sterile environment, avoiding infection and allowing the beer to condition for the right period before declaring it ready to drink.

Once you've mastered that, and you progress through adding successive bits of kit that turn your home brew set-up into a mini-version of a real brewery, the entire world of brewing is at your fingertips.

The *future*
of good beer

Ok, so it's the best time there's ever been to drink beer. But can something this good possibly last?

As a beer writer and pundit, there's one question I get asked more than any other: is the current craft beer boom a bubble? And if so, is that bubble about to burst?

People started asking that question in the UK sometime back around 2011-2012, so it's curious that they're still asking it now. Bubbles are transient, whereas craft beer gives every impression of settling in and making itself comfortable.

Here's the business bit: the number of breweries in Britain has pretty much quadrupled since the Millennium, and the pace of new openings is increasing, not slowing down. A quarter of British adults – about 13 million people – say they drink craft beer, even if they're not quite sure what the term means or if it's much use or not. And craft beer has gone global: research suggests there are now more than 10,000 craft breweries in over 200 countries. Looking at the research, in each country this author knows something about, the total number of breweries listed seems to be a dramatic understatement.

In America, craft beer has been around as a potent force for nearly forty years. The children of the first wave of craft brewers are now opening breweries of their own.

Some 'bubble'.

It seems unlikely that, once millions of people have acquired a taste for flavourful beers – hop-forward, barrel-aged or spontaneously fermented – they'll suddenly decide *en masse* that they're bored of all this variety and revert back to pints of Stella and Foster's with a lemonade top. Or that, having discovered that some people would rather pay £5 or £6 for a pint of flavourful, well made beer instead of £3 for some soulless, tasteless factory product, clever brewers will revert to a policy of 'churn it out, pile it high and sell it cheap'.

But these aren't the real worries of those who ask if craft beer is a bubble. Before we get to a point where craft beer disappears completely, there's the worry that it might lose its heart and soul; that just like punk or any other form of cultural rebellion, it might be subsumed by the corporate machine it set itself against, and be turned into mere product.

There are certainly justifiable grounds for such worries. Big brewers see their business threatened by craft brewers, and they wouldn't be doing their jobs properly if they didn't respond to that threat. If beer drinkers turn to a big global corporation and say, "Your beer is bland and characterless so we're going over here to drink this guy's beer instead," you can hardy blame them for listening and starting to brew more characterful beers themselves. Listening to the consumer and responding to their needs is how they got to be so big in the first place.

Well, that and corporate skulduggery. And that's where the real concern lies.

If you have colossal amount of money but no creativity or soul, it makes perfect sense to buy a successful craft brewery for far more than it's actually worth. At best you get the future of brewing; at worst you remove a pesky threat.

And this is where it gets tricky: we're in the middle of a spate of craft brewers 'selling out' to big corporates, and those that do are routinely condemned by beer pundits, especially if they've previously asserted their commitment to independence and 'keeping it real'.

But when someone like Anheuser-Busch Inbev comes knocking with its chequebook, it's invariably offering the craft brewery owners far more money than they could ever make from their brewery as a going concern. Most craft beer drinkers are affluent professionals who almost certainly earn more than the independent brewer they love, who has three mortgages on her house and works ninety hours a week. It's a bit much for these people to insist that brewer should remain poor and overworked so they can feel comfortably anti-establishment once they clock off at 6pm.

However, it is worrying for the independent spirit of craft beer if lots of small brewers sell out to the majors. Apart from your favourite brand selling out, consolidation gives the big boys power over sourcing ingredients and owning distribution, with the danger being they'll be able to freeze smaller players out of the market.

But for every brewer that sells out, there are more that want to remain fiercely independent, and a seemingly unstoppable wave of new entrants. Big corporations can't help but be risk averse, and there's a market for that – safe beers from familiar brands that help pull people into 'crafty' beers for the first time. Once they're there, there's a much bigger chance they'll then move on to true craft beers from small producers, and everyone wins. This is what happened in cider a decade ago, when the success of Magner's – a big, corporate brand that most purists wouldn't consider to be 'real' cider at all – had a dramatic knock-on effect that lifted the fortunes of traditional farmhouse cider makers, whose businesses had been on their deathbeds a couple of years previously.

Craft beer will change in size and shape, and the word 'craft' may or may nor eventually lose its usefulness, as some argue it already has. But drinkers face a bright future of better beer.

Right now, hardcore craft brewers and drinkers – some of them alarmed perhaps by the mainstreaming of IPA – are pushing flavour and style into uncharted waters, seeing how far it can go. Barrel ageing, experimentation with wild yeasts and the addition of ingredients that have never been in beer before are performing like experiments always do: many of the results are dreadful failures, but there's always the chance of something that revolutionises our lives. And with every trend comes a counter trend: the biggest trends in America right now are session IPAs that people can and will drink a few pints of without falling over, and a move back to lager – well-made, flavourful lager like the Czechs make, but clean and fresh enough to please a palate that's not quite ready for a hop bomb – or has had enough of hop bombs for the time being.

It's still the best time there's ever been to be a beer drinker. I've actually been saying that for ten years now, and I'm still saying it, because it keeps getting better. I think we'll all be saying it for a good while yet.

Glossary

ALPHA ACIDS

Secreted by the lupulin glands of the hop cone, Alpha Acids are crucial to the flavour of most beers. When heated, they form iso-alpha acids (a process called isomerisation), which have a characteristic bitterness.

BARREL

Most barrels used for ageing beer are made of oak, which is both watertight and imparts desirable flavours and aromas. As well as fresh barrels, brewers often take wood from other industries, for example wine, whisky and brandy, depending on the character they are trying to achieve.

MACROBREWING

Large-scale, industrial brewing. While macro-scale brewers arguably have their own craft, the term is often used to set 'cheap', low-quality, mass-produced beers apart from more complex micro-brewed fare.

BLENDING

Batches of beer are often combined to reach a target flavour profile. The term 'blending' is mostly associated with barrel-aged or spontaneously fermented beers.

BOIL

The section of the brewing process where the wort is boiled vigorously to trigger certain chemical changes, including isomerisation.

BRETTANOMYCES

Translating literally as "British yeast" brettanomyces – or 'brett' – is more commonly associated with Belgian brewing. It produces considerable amounts of acetic acid, so can often be found in sour beers, though it is also responsible for other characteristics including 'funky' flavours and aromas.

CAMRA

The Campaign for Real Ale, established in 1971 to combat the perceived threat of macrobrewing – and specifically lager – to Britain's real ale brewing tradition. Since the rise of craft beer in the UK, the organisation has sought to modernise and ensure its relevance to a new generation of beer lovers.

CASK

Cask beer is unfiltered, unpasteurised and undergoes a secondary fermentation inside a cask, to be served without the addition of carbon dioxide or nitrogen. Subtle, rounded and naturally effervescent (generally less bubbly than kegged beer) cask ales are a distinctly British phenomenon, and a source of fierce pride for a certain subset of UK beer lovers. Because of the 'live' nature of cask ales, they tend to be more sensitive to mistreatment, and the art of storing and serving cask is considered something of an art form.

CARBON DIOXIDE

A natural by-product of the fermentation process (alongside alcohol) carbon dioxide (CO_2) gas is highly soluble in water (or beer) and is what gives your pint its fizz. Once poured, bubbles of CO_2 coalesce around microscopic imperfections on the surface of the glass and rise up to form a head. Unless a beer is cask or bottle-conditioned, it's likely to have been 'force-carbonated', meaning the CO_2 is added after fermentation. Although it's a source of passionate disagreement, there's no evidence that force-carbonated beer is materially different to naturally carbonated beer.

CONDITIONING

A vital step in many beers, which occurs at the end of fermentation. Having done the job of converting sugar to alcohol and CO_2, the remaining yeast sets to work eating up other less desirable by-products, which might otherwise lead to off-flavours in the finished beer. Thanks yeast.

COOLSHIP
A large, flat open fermentation vessel that invites yeast and other micro-organisms present in the environment to infect the wort.

COPPER
The vessel used for boiling the wort.

ENZYMES
Enzymes are complex biological catalysts; essentially microscopic powerhouses for speeding up chemical reactions. In the brewing process, the enzymes found naturally on the husks of malted grain activate during mashing, at around 64 degrees Celcius, and work furiously to convert the starches and other long-chain carbohydrates around the kernel into sweet, fermentable sugar.

ESSENTIAL OILS
The fresh, aromatic, juicy compounds that we love in our modern hoppy beers. Since these are driven off quickly during the boil, 'aroma' hops are generally added late, or even after the boil, to retain some of these delicious characteristics.

FILTERING
There are many different techniques used to filter beer, and many different reasons for doing so. Whatever the current trend, it's important to remember that filtering isn't automatically a good thing, or a bad thing, and that a bright beer isn't necessarily filtered.

HOPS
A botanically unusual structure, hops are part cone, part

flower, and can be found growing throughout the world's warm temperate regions. Most closely related to hemp and nettles, they've been used in brewing for hundreds of years (starting in Flanders) initially for their antiseptic properties, which made beer last longer. Hops are highly regional, and each growing region has its own distinctive varieties and styles from the subtle noble hops of Germany to the brash and juicy hops of America and New Zealand.

HYDROMETER
A simple measuring device for testing the 'gravity' of a liquid. The more sugar is dissolved in the beer, the higher the hydrometer floats. By knowing both the 'original gravity' and the 'final gravity' it is possible to calculate how much sugar has been converted to alcohol during fermentation (some sugar molecules are too large to convert) and therefore what the beers ABV is.

LACTOBACILLUS
A very useful bacterium that converts sugar into lactic acid, and is therefore a key ingredient in many sour beers.

MALTED BARLEY
The tried-and-tested number one source of fermentable sugar in brewing (as well as contributing flavour, aroma, colour, texture and so on). During malting, barley seeds are given the heat and moisture they need to begin germinating. This kicks off a complex chemical process, whereby the long carbohydrates stored around the grain's kernel begin to break down into the more useful, energy-packed sugars the seed will need in its early hours and days. Once this is just underway, the grains are lightly toasted and dried to stop germination in its tracks, leaving the sugars available for brewing.

MASHING

During mashing, grains are soaked in temperature controlled water, activating the enzymes on their husks and releasing their valuably sugar content. To ensure as much sugar as possible is captured from the grain (this is referred to as the brew's 'efficiency') more warm water is usually sprayed over it.

PROGRESSIVE BEER DUTY

Introduced by Gordon Brown in 2002, Progressive Beer Duty gives small brewers a vital tax break, helping them compete on slightly more even terms with the big boys. It has arguably played a major role in the UK's craft beer revolution.

SECONDARY FERMENTATION

Once primary fermentation is complete, some beers are given an extra shot of fermentable sugar in their serving vessel – usually bottle or cask – to momentarily perk up the yeast in suspension and provide the CO2 for a little fizz.

WORT

The sweet, malty liquid resulting from the mashing stage of any brew.

YEAST

The undisputed star of beer-making, this single-celled organic miracle takes sugary water and breaks it down into gas and alcohol. There are many different species of yeast found abundantly in nature – in the air, on the skins of fruit – and some of these have been isolated and cultivated over the centuries to behave in specific ways and produce specific characteristics. From cloves to bananas and bubblegum, the range of flavours and aromas that yeast can produce underthe right conditions is truly breathtaking.

Index

About the author
Pete Brown

Regular contributor to Beer52's *Ferment* magazine,
Pete Brown is a British writer who specialises in making
people thirsty. He has previously authored eight books
and wrote the annual Cask Report for its first nine years.
He writes numerous articles in the drinks trade press and
consumer press, for the likes of The Guardian.

He appears regularly on TV and radio, and has judged
competitions including the BBC Food and Farming Awards,
the Great Taste Awards and the Great British Pub Awards.
He's a member of the British Guild of Beer Writers, and was
named Beer Writer of the Year in 2009, 2012 and 2016.

About the illustrator
Jay Daniel Wright

Jay Daniel Wright makes bold and colourful work full of
fun and sometimes slightly shifty characters, perfectly
fusing the comic and classic to create his precise,
distinctive style.

Originally from England but now living in Berlin, Jay's
previous life as a carpenter left him with a meticulousness
that means he is never far away from a pencil and ruler.

You can follow his work on Instagram: @jaydanielwright

The Story of *Craft* Beer

First published in 2017 by Beer52

Beer52
26 Howe Street
Edinburgh
EH3 6TG

Designer: Ashley Johnston

ISBN: 978-1-5272-1214-5